Dressed to Perfection

Dressed to Perfection

The Art of Dressing
for Your
Red Carpet Moments

Carmen Marc Valvo

WITH HOLLY HABER

CONTRIBUTIONS BY KATIE COURIC
& VANESSA WILLIAMS

RIZZOLI NEW YORK

Contents

FOREWORD
By Katie Couric

I love Carmen Marc Valvo. I love him as a person, and I love him as a designer. I love the way he works with fabric—the colors and the textures—and understands how it drapes and flatters and makes every woman feel like a million bucks. I know I do. His craftsmanship, timeless sense of style, and elegance are unparalled. He creates beautiful and comfortable dresses that make real women red-carpet ready. And for that, we are all grateful.

But most of all, I love Carmen Marc Valvo for his commitment to the cause that I, too, champion: colon cancer education, prevention, and research.

This cause is personal for me because my husband, Jay Monahan, died of colon cancer at the age of only 42. It's personal for Carmen, too. Carmen insisted on getting tested for colon cancer when he was 48, two years earlier than the recommended screening age. He just felt something wasn't right. That test revealed that Carmen had cancer. Had he not insisted on getting screened, he might not be with us today. Because he did, he was able to get the treatment he needed and was cured. Carmen is literally living proof that early detection saves lives.

Despite his busy life and hectic schedule, Carmen has devoted an extraordinary amount of time and energy to spreading the word that colon cancer can be cured if detected early, and often prevented entirely with appropriate screening. He has been extremely generous to the National Colorectal Cancer Research Alliance (NCCRA), which I co-founded with the Entertainment Industry Foundation. Carmen

and the always-glamorous Vanessa Williams appeared in a public service announcement together, making the point that "there's nothing glamorous about colon cancer," and urging people to get screened.

Carmen shares my determination to make it fashionable to talk about colon cancer. And who better than one of America's favorite designers to deliver that message? Especially to women, who often underestimate their risk for this disease, which strikes men and women in equal numbers. In 2006, it was my pleasure to present Carmen with NCCRA's first Advocate Award in recognition of his commitment to the cause.

Carmen Marc Valvo knows how to make women look and feel fabulous on the outside. But he also cares deeply about how we feel on the inside. So, please, take his advice. If you are fifty years of age or older, get screened for colon cancer. If you are under fifty, consult your doctor about whether your family history warrants getting screened. And if someone you love is fifty or older, remind him or her that taking care of their health never goes out of style.

Opposite: Katie Couric, 2010 Costume Institute Gala
Previous page left: Satin face silk organza "Magnolia" dress

Carmen–of Course!

By Vanessa Williams

Where do I start with Carmen Marc Valvo? I've been having a love affair with Carmen's designs for almost twenty years. There's a signature Carmen look that always gets you noticed on the red carpet. I wear Carmen so often that when other celebrities come up to me at events and ask, "who are you wearing?" and I answer "Carmen," they say, "of course!" Carmen's dresses have always made me feel elegant and feminine. His silhouettes give me the confidence to perform on stage, pose on the red carpet, and feel confident on television.

However, it's more than the designer—it's the man who Carmen is that makes him so endearing to me. Carmen is genuine, generous, and gracious—a wonderful person as well as a gifted artist. His commitment to cancer awareness is admirable and his commitment to making women look and feel truly beautiful is exceptional. In a field where too many designers seek to mold women into their designs, Carmen stands out as a designer who loves women–and really loves to make them look gorgeous. I've been very fortunate to have Carmen on my side for many years, and I'm thrilled to see him thrive with such a long list of fans in Hollywood and all over the world. He is a brilliant designer, and an extraordinary man who deserves it.

Carmen and Vanessa Williams, 2008 CFDA Awards

Introduction

by Holly Haber

I knew Carmen Marc Valvo through his dresses long before I met the man himself.

They arrived regularly in brown boxes for fashion shoots at the Dallas branch of *Women's Wear Daily*. My assistant and I always opened them with a thrill of anticipation because we knew something beautiful would be inside. Carmen's samples were consistently stunning; they fit, and they photographed beautifully, producing an image that always met the exacting standards of my editors in New York.

Thousands of other women have a similar relationship with Carmen from afar—they rely on him to make them look good. He is one of those rare designers who creates fashion that is timely as well as timeless and luxurious but never overwrought.

Many designers instantly concentrate on the most expensive tier of the market, dressing women who are able to part with thousands of dollars for a dress. Carmen launched his company in 1989 by focusing on the more numerous, equally deserving women who could splurge hundreds of dollars to look their best.

His design sensibility, however, was top notch—so much so that celebrities began choosing to wear his dresses over more expensive frocks. Demand from stars and stylists prompted him to create in 1997 Carmen Marc Valvo Couture, a more extravagant red carpet collection at a higher price point. It was a reversal of the industry norm, in which a designer makes a name with pricey styles and then produces a lower-priced label for wider distribution.

Today, both Carmen Marc Valvo Collection and Couture are successful at Neiman Marcus, Saks Fifth Avenue, Bloomingdale's, and Nordstrom, and fine stores nationwide. He has expanded into other areas, such as swimwear, always with an accent on

Ruffled strapless gowns in silk organza, Spring 2011 collection

glamour. Carmen is so important to Neiman's that company chairman and chief executive officer Karen Katz makes it a point to attend his runway show each season, as does Ken Downing, senior vice president and fashion director.

"Carmen allows a woman to have her own 'red carpet moment' every time she wears one of his creations," Downing says. "His understanding of the elegant and the glamorous make him a very popular designer with our customers."

Carmen Marc Valvo. The name sounds so exotic that Carmen has been accused of christening himself to buttress his brand. But Carmen is neither foreign nor a pretender. His parents named him according to family tradition, and he grew up in affluent Westchester County, N.Y., the eldest son of an anesthesiologist and a nurse.

Carmen considered a career in medicine, but he had always loved art. He got his first set of oil paints when he was nine. After dabbling in fine art and architecture, including study in Europe, he returned to New York and had an epiphany.

"I said, 'fashion! I'm going to do it,'" Carmen recalled during our interviews for this book. He worked his way through Parsons School of Design by waiting tables, and then landed plum assistant positions at Nina Ricci, Christian Dior, and other fashion firms before starting his own company.

Carmen's approach is old school—to make exquisite, refined clothes that accentuate the women who wear them. He has none of the imperious designer attitude that has become an unfortunate cliché of the industry.

Carmen is witty and humble and approachable, which is partly why his clients love him so much. He's not afraid to admit that he wore ridiculous platform boots in the '70s, or that he was starstruck when he met Angela Lansbury. He rescues cats—he and his partner of thirty-five years, Christian Knaust, have four tabbies that they lovingly tote along for weekends in their cozy Bridgehampton home.

Christian, who runs the business and is a trained designer himself, is also a giving and amiable soul, the sort of host who treats guests to a special bottle of wine from the cellar. Both Carmen and Christian are the go-to experts for weddings for their families, right down to fixing a bride's botched hairstyle at the last minute.

It's this generosity of spirit that motivates Carmen to give every client, from the household names who come to his New York showroom to the loyal customers he meets in stores, careful attention to her individual needs and desires. Carmen is always looking to make woman shine.

Opposite: Carmen with Taylor and Nicole, finale of Fall 2005 runway show
Following pages: Fall 2005 runway show

"*A beautiful woman can turn heads but real glamour has a deeper pull . . . Glamour [is] the power to rearrange people's emotions.*"

—Arthur Miller

Making Women Shine

Achieving Star-Quality Glamour

In my early childhood, I was constantly surrounded by women—my mother, grandmother, and three sisters. My father, an anesthesiologist, was seldom around due to his grueling hospital schedule, and my two brothers weren't born until much later in my life. For almost five years of my early existence, I was exclusively in the company of women, and perhaps this is where my love affair with fashion began.

My mother was a very stylish woman who was passionate about dressing. There was artistry in how she pulled together a look. This was the '50s—the halcyon days of the American Dream—a time when women were so very glamorous and captivating. Women really dressed in that era; they dressed to celebrate life. I recall countless pairs of gloves, and incredible collections of hats, shoes, and glorious jewelry—how my mother loved bijoux. I remember her fantastic straw hat with pheasant feathers, and a wonderful pair of metallic leather mules that mysteriously stayed on her feet even when she wore stockings.

My grandmother, a seamstress, was constantly buzzing along on a sewing machine. As a child, I remember watching her for hours, mesmerized by the constant movement of her hands and her seemingly magical ability to turn pieces of fabric into a fantastic dress or other article of clothing. She seemed always to be in her bedroom creating something of beauty for my mother and sisters. I suspect the time I spent with her and the constant hum of her machine must have embedded itself in my subconscious, influencing my later work.

Pleated silk lamé gown—also worn by Beyoncé Knowles, Fall 2003 collection

Embrace Glamour Everyday

My first attempt at dress design was for my sister's school project, an assignment with a Renaissance theme. I was nine at the time, and I dressed her Barbie doll collection in my own creations. The sole remaining piece from that effort is a black-and-white polka-dot gown with leg-o'-mutton sleeves and a matching cone hat with a chiffon train. The fabric may have been wrong, but the silhouette was correct! I've framed that whimsical dress in a shadow box that I keep in my office, and to this day, it still makes me smile.

As a child of the '50s, I was very influenced by the golden era of Hollywood. I adored all those cinematic extravaganzas with their captivating leading ladies and that famous Hollywood style—the gamine quality of Audrey Hepburn, the regal aura of Grace Kelly, the fire of Rita Hayworth, and the sultriness of Lena Horne. And, of course, I would be remiss not to mention the gorgeous Marilyn Monroe. These women are legendary icons of style, and I am still moved by their glamour and beauty.

The inimitable sparkle of these leading ladies imbued my soul with a sense of glamour, which has shaped who I am. I think that's why I am so enamored with evening wear. Every woman, at some time in her life, wants to make a Hollywood entrance in a spectacular gown that exudes style and sensuality, just like a star. Every woman deserves to be in the spotlight.

Although the occasion for dressing in evening attire does not occur as often as I would like, I don't believe that this is any reason not to infuse a bit of glamour into everyday life. *A sensational pair of sunglasses or an elegant swimsuit can elevate your spirits and fill your soul with a little star quality.*

Above: Audrey Hepburn wearing the classic and sleek black dress in Breakfast at Tiffany's, *1961*

Opposite: The halter dress worn by Marilyn Monroe in 1955 will always be in style

Following pages: Glamorous looks from Carmen's runways for all occasions

20

Beauty has always been in the eye of the beholder, and its ideal has changed over centuries. From the porcelain complexion and flowing tresses of Botticelli's Venus; to the statuesque beauties Rubens so loved to paint; to the strength and angularity of Tamara de Lempicka's women; the female figure has been celebrated in many incarnations over the millennia. It is my belief that beauty comes in all colors, shapes, and sizes.

Above: Silk duchess satin strapless ball gown, Fall 2005 collection
Opposite: Ashley Judd, Spring 1994 Advertising Campaign

Refining Features

We all have our own perception of who we are. But when we look in the mirror, we never see ourselves as other people do because we are only looking at a reflection that does not portray us accurately. If you think about it, the mirror's reflection is a likeness in reverse. Women tend to be very hard on themselves and unnecessarily so.

These perceived flaws are never that important or noticeable. People look at a distorted mirror and make harsh judgments about themselves without really seeing the whole picture. *There are so many ways to minimize our least favorite features through the way we dress and, in kind, to enhance our best ones.*

While it may not seem like it, celebrities have insecurities about their appearance just like everyone else. They are constantly being photographed and critiqued, which forces them to become highly selective and discerning about their wardrobes. *They have learned how to accentuate their finer features while camouflaging others, which is exactly what we should all strive to do.* Celebrities have become extremely aware of their posture, for example, and of how they stand and walk on the red carpet. They turn slightly to the side for photographs, which is slimming to the silhouette, rather than facing the camera straight on. Each has learned which is his or her best side and naturally turns that side toward the camera—a technique everyone can employ for their own red-carpet moments. And, of course, they are always smiling.

Proportion is the primary means to achieving a perfect balance to your appearance. It can be adjusted by adding volume to strategic areas. For instance, a dress with just a little swag of chiffon that moves around the skirt can minimize the bust and give new volume to the hip. Similarly, a beautifully draped bodice will add volume to the bust, when needed. *Diagonal and linear strokes automatically create a look of verticality, elongating the wearer.* Knowing some of these clever deceptions will allow you to wear them well.

Grace Kelly remains the epitome of glamour and elegance

All of the women who I've met over the years have enabled me to perfect my craft. From coast to coast and from north to south, I've traveled to many cities and have met women from all over our great nation. Women are my muses. There is nothing as beautiful to me as the female form; it is the perfect curvilinear canvas. Women are the ones who continue to inspire me—their needs, their sorrows, and most importantly, their triumphs.

Above: Black guipure lace strapless cocktail dress, Spring 2007 collection
Opposite: Maria Menounos in a satin appliqué gown at the Cannes Film Festival

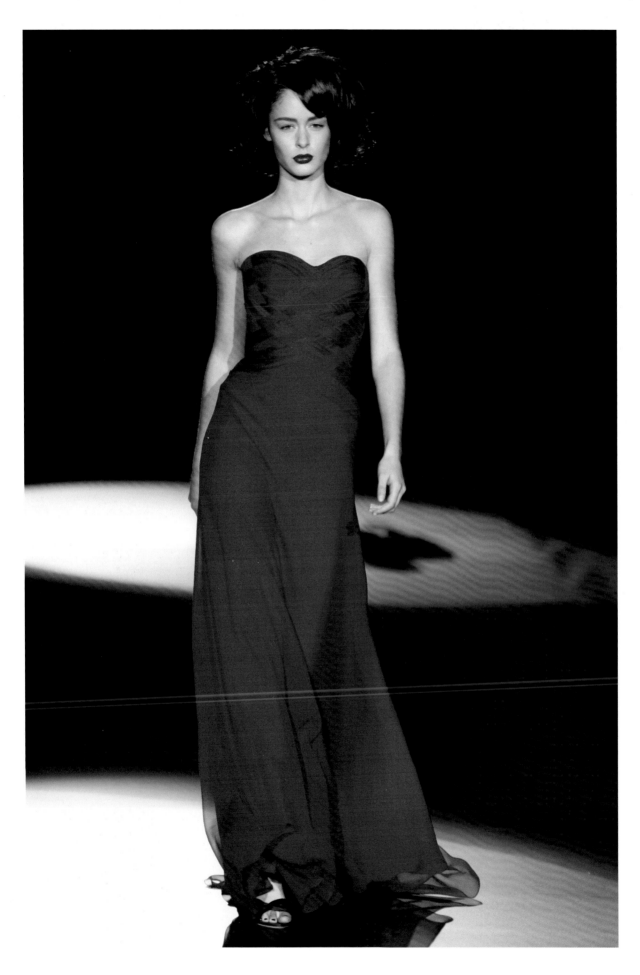

Above: Satin and crepe gown, Fall 2006 collection
Opposite: Rita Hayworth, 1946

CREATING STYLE
Finding Your Fashion Muse

Originating from the mythology of ancient Greece, the Muses were known as the lovely goddesses who gracefully sang, danced, and played music—inspiring others to do the same. There are various legends—one story deems them water nymphs who sprang from sacred streams while another claims the Muses as the nine daughters of Zeus— all of the stories attribute the divine inspiration of these otherworldly women as the impetus for the creation of art and culture.

What is a muse today? I like to say, jokingly, that it is someone who is amusing! But essentially that is true. A muse can be enlightening and entertaining, with the amazing gift of firing up the imaginations of others. A muse might be someone you admire, as many of the Hollywood icons we've mentioned, or it could simply be a state of mind. Over the course of the millennia, the concept of the muse has evolved and taken so many different forms that it's not surprising that it can mean different things to different people.

To a designer, a muse is someone or something that incites the creation of something new and exciting. The inspiration can be as astounding as the mystical colors of sunset over the Serengeti, or as the simple undulating motion of a tree in the wind that the designer seeks to capture and re-create in a new form. Ultimately, however, most fashion designers find their greatest sources of inspiration in real women whom they personally know and respect. Consider the long-lasting relationship between Yves Saint Laurent and Loulou de la Falaise, or Halston and the effervescent Pat Cleveland.

Chiffon with pearl embroidery, Spring 2008 collection

Carmen's Muse

Taylor Foster has been my muse for over a decade. The relationship between a designer and muse is a very close one; you put complete faith in that person's judgment, allowing them to serve almost as an alter ego. Working this closely with a muse is like dancing a tango. It can be slow and moody or fiery and passionate, submissive or aggressive. And sometimes when you dance with your muse in perfect harmony, magic is created.

The process begins with the initial idea. The fabric is draped onto a manne-quin, pinned to perfection, and then engineered onto a flat paper pattern. From there, fabric is cut to match the paper pattern and sewn into the first sample prototype. Then it's ready to be slipped onto a woman, and the anticipation begins.

Above, opposite, and following pages: Preparing for Fashion Week, Fall 2005

The Perfect Fit

When Taylor tries a sample dress and walks to the giant mirror at the end of the hall in my showroom, I may notice her expression or walk change ever so slightly, and her eyes and face begin to glow. It's an almost imperceptible nuance, but when the dress is perfection, she transforms and a certain sensuality emerges. That's what I want to do for every woman.

A wonderful dress can infuse a woman with a confidence and inner beauty, empowering the way she moves and feels. There is nothing on earth that gives me more pleasure than to see that glow in a woman wearing one of my designs.

Walk . . . Walk . . . Walk . . . I learned how critical that walk was while working as an assistant designer in the houses of Nina Ricci and Christian Dior in Paris. As Taylor tries on each dress, I ask her to walk the long hallway so I can see the gown in motion. Her walk usually gives me a startlingly accurate portrayal of how other women will look and feel in my design.

Obviously, when you try on a dress, it is important to look at your reflection in a mirror for your initial impression. But there is much more to consider. You must observe the design from all angles.

A dress should make a striking first impression and a lasting departing one. *When choosing a dress for your red-carpet moment, be sure to experience it while walking, dancing, and sitting.* You will see how the dress moves and how you give life to the dress. You will see yourself unite with the dress and become a vision of beauty.

Above: Cocktail dress in silk organza, Spring 2007 collection

Opposite: Gown in silk organza, Spring 2007 collection

International Fashion

My mother was born in the small town of Cosenza in Calabria, Italy. My father's origins are a bit more enigmatic. How I loved spending summers in Rome as a child. Everyone was so impressed when I told them, until they finally found out it was Rome, New York, where my father was born. His father, however, was born in Palermo, Sicily, and his grandfather in Sardinia. It seems my paternal forefathers were into island hopping. We can trace my lineage further back from Sardinia to Corsica to perhaps somewhere in the north of Spain, where the thread gets lost—so maybe a sense of wanderlust is inherent in my DNA.

I have visited nearly every continent, and countless countries therein. These experiences have not only shaped me as a person but have also had a huge impact on my design philosophy. By traveling, you are able to discover so much about different peoples and customs—their clothing, art, and unique cultural icons. *The more you travel, the more these experiences enable you to envision new perspectives and will inevitably inspire you to embrace new fashions, fabrics, silhouettes, and colors into your wardrobe.*

Above: Silk chiffon with Zardozi beading (detail), Fall 1997 collection
Opposite: Silk lamé halter gown (detail), Fall 2004 collection

Silk Organza & the Obi Sash

I have always been intrigued with origami—the Japanese folk art of folding paper into sculptures resembling cranes, butterflies, and other creatures. There is something very precise about this craft, but poetic at the same time. I have translated some of these techniques into the manipulation of strips of silk organza. I love how relaxing this simple action can be, transforming folds of fabric into a single floral bud for a bodice, or creating cascades of waterfalls rippling down the back of a white wedding gown.

While designing my Fall 2003 collection, I became enamored with the concept of the obi sash. This waist-defining belt became a pivotal point of the collection, minimizing the midsection of a woman's body. I used patent leather with an origami flourish to achieve my desired result. *While traveling, if you are able to procure such a fabulous piece as a vintage obi sash, I would highly recommend incorporating that article of clothing into your everyday wardrobe.* Wear it with a crisp linen shirt and a pair of jeans or a fabulous blouse and an evening ball-gown skirt.

Above: Midnight gazar gown, Spring 2008 collection
Opposite: Carmen's take on the obi sash in pleated silk

Embroidery & the Tunic

Another place that I'm passionate about is the Indian subcontinent. I love its spicy fragrances of saffron and curry, its glorious colors, and its extraordinary art. India is a magical place. One of the first collections we showed at the tents of Bryant Park during Fashion Week was inspired by the colors and craftsmanship of India. I drew inspiration from the paisley motif and the use of elaborate Zardosi metal embroidery and beadwork, and I tried to emulate the exoticism, mystery, and sensuality of the subcontinent. The proportion of the Indian churidar is an ideal example of cross cultural influences. *The side-slit tunic, which falls to mid-thigh or mid-calf, is worn over slim pants or leggings, much like today's tunics.* Simple and elegant, it slenderizes and elongates the body. It is a perfect proportion, especially for more Rubenesque figures.

The Bangle Bracelet

One could accent their look with jewelry inspired by India or Asia, like the bangle bracelet—how glorious it is in bone or ivory or inlayed with ebony and metal. The bangle is the one piece of jewelry that can be a welcome addition to so many different ensembles.

Above and opposite: Printed silk mousseline gown, Spring 2006 collection

Above: Micro pleated metallic
lace empire gown, Spring
2008 collection

Opposite: Crystal pleated
lace spiral gown, Spring
2008 collection

Beyond the Sea

Another important inspiration in my work has always been the ocean—I'm enamored with the deep blue sea and the endless waves rippling across it. I love incorporating these images into my designs. *You can draw inspiration from many different aspects of the shore to create an ensemble that is unique and beautiful just for you.* For instance, you may employ the idea of the shell to play with color or the shape of your outfit, like I did for one of my spring collections after a visit to the Maldive Islands. No matter what you see as your muse, you must allow room for experimentation to create a look that is your own.

Your Personal Monogram

A muse will help you keep your ensembles fresh and unexpected. You must always strive to develop your own fashion calling card, whether you choose to be inspired by the little black dresses of the revered style icon Audrey Hepburn or embrace a quirky accessory like the signature eyeglasses of the legendary Iris Apfel. *You may even find your personal look by indulging in a classic piece such as Grace Kelly's eponymous Kelly bag to move your look from the everyday to the iconoclastic.*

Finding your perfect dress is only the beginning to discovering an incredible world of fashion possibilities open to you. Now you must take that dress and personalize it. *Whether you choose to showcase a treasured piece of jewelry or tie a scarf ever so beautifully and adorn it with myriad vintage brooches, you will elevate the dress by making it your own.* Remember, you must always look forward . . . never look back. You must find yourself amused!

Above left: Origami folded crepe cocktail, Fall 2007 collection
Above right: Pleated petal embroidered cocktail dress, Spring 2007 collection
Opposite: Organza blouse and pinstripe wool sateen pant, Spring 2008 collection

THE ARCHITECTURE OF FASHION
Building Your Look

Architectural design—be it the Parthenon or an ultramodern structure such as I. M. Pei's Pyramide du Louvre—is always made up of a myriad of elements. But architecture, no matter how magnificent, has only the three dimensions: height, width, and depth. Even sculpture, unless it's a mobile, has a mere three dimensions. In fashion, however, a fourth dimension comes into play—movement.

Movement is also a key element in a garden where flowers, leaves, and branches are caressed by the wind. That is one of the reasons why my garden is such an inspiration to me—and why designing a beautiful gown is such a delightful experience. It is the movement, the sensuous undulation, that transforms the final design—elevating a simple black dress to a true work of art.

There are other aspects, of course—shape, color, and texture, for instance—that make a dress come alive. When all of these elements come together harmoniously, there is nothing quite as breathtaking as a woman in a dazzling gown gliding gracefully across a room.

Throughout history, the art and architecture of various cultures have profoundly influenced fashion. The ancient Greeks, for example, defined beauty in human terms and created what they believed was the perfect figure. This ideal physique has literally transcended time as artists re-interpret it over and over again. Consider the *Venus de Milo* or Michelangelo's perfectly proportioned *David* or Rodin's *The Kiss*, and you begin to see that archetype and how it recurs and evolves.

Dress in pleated silk ribbon and feathers, Fall 2008 collection

Behind the Design

In truth, fashion designers must be architects and mathematicians as well. We must always consider the proportions of the wearer and what would be most flattering to her. On occasion I use a tape measure, and sometimes a calculator, to arrive at the precise numbers required to properly execute a design that enhances the female form. *I have always maintained that the most minimalist style belies the complexity of its true nature.* Often, when designing my gowns, I will actually build from the inside out.

All designs begin with a solid foundation made of building blocks from which the dress will emerge. Although ruching is one of my signatures, it is most important that I first construct the framework for the drape by using layers and layers of foundation. The heart and soul of the design must be created before the drape can be perfected.

This same approach informs all of my collections, especially my swim line. A draped swimsuit may seem like a relatively simple affair; actually, it requires layers of foundation as well as a few other secret weapons to give it a fabulous fit.

I'm a classicist at heart. My designs reflect a certain refinement, subtle elegance, and a feeling of timelessness, which may be directly related to my background in fine arts. *For me, design is all about texture—choosing the ideal fabrics—and the right colors.* I might start with chiffon and then build the color into a different hue with another layer of chiffon and then top it all off with a piece of intricately woven lace, like layers and layers of paint on a canvas, with a sprinkling of beads to finish the composition of the dress.

Above: Black satin faced organza ball gown, Fall 2007 collection
Opposite: Tiered silk organza cocktail dress, Fall 2007 collection

Perfecting Proportions

In fashion, as in classical Greek sculpture, proportion is paramount. The ideal feminine proportion in ancient Greece was based on the number seven, in which the height of a woman's head was about one-seventh of the body's length. My fashion sketches embody an idealized "high-fashion" proportion in which the head is one-ninth of the length of the figure, the torso is one-third, and the legs are an exaggerated five-ninths.

As we all know, women's bodies are gloriously different. A designer will try to create the illusion of perfect proportion or visually elongate the body, which enhances most figures, by adapting some centuries-old couturiers' "tricks" such as a regal empire waistline, which is always slenderizing and elongating, or the artful use of draping, which camouflages and enhances at the same time.

Tiered silk organza cocktail dress, Fall 2007 collection

Elongating Silhouettes

The empire silhouette is a perfect example of one such illusion. With its abbreviated bodice nipped in snugly under the bust, the silhouette changes the proportion of the body and creates an elongated, elegant look accentuating vertical lines.

My most alluring silhouettes are those in which the eye is inexorably drawn to the décolletage, such as soft draping that flows over the bust to the waist; or ruching, in which fabric is gathered, then anchored down with tiny stitches secretly hidden within the folds stopping just below the bust. Both of these styles are immensely flattering and they work on many diverse figure types.

Above left: Silk jersey gown, Spring 2009 collection
Above right: Basket weave silk satin faced chiffon gown, Spring 2009 collection

Above left: Zardozi embroidered silk satin gown, Spring 2007 collection
Above right: Silk chiffon ribbon and baby sequin gown, Spring 2007 collection

The Dramatic Bias-Cut

Another way to create a visual lengthening of the body line is to wear anything cut on the bias, which is when the garment is cut on the diagonal of the fabric's grain. The bias-cut is as effective on a dramatic, one-shoulder gown as on a simple day dress. Created by Madeleine Vionnet, who opened her Paris fashion house in 1912 and became one of the world's greatest couturiers, the bias cut gracefully follows the lines of the body, reminiscent of classical Greek sculpture. Vionnet's masterpieces, created by hand, resulted in a wonderfully fluid movement that celebrated the feminine form in all its glory. Her dresses have inspired me and many other designers, such as the incomparable Halston and John Galliano

What I adore so much about bias-cut designs is that they mold and conform so perfectly to the wearer's individual body type. The bias cut is almost like an elastic encasement to a woman's particular form. It expands when needed to envelope more ample proportions, and retracts when necessary. It is one of the most easily worn and flattering silhouettes.

Above: Sleeveless Vioneet gowns, 1930
Opposite: Bias-cut gowns, Fall 1992 advertising campaign

Discover Draping

There is nothing quite as sensuous and flattering on a woman as draping, which involves a simple length of fabric that is artfully wrapped around the body. This ancient art references the popular styles worn in Roman times when women wore a *stola*, a long, columnlike dress accompanied by a long rectangular shawl called a *palla*. Commonly worn draped over one shoulder and around the back, the palla helped elongate the figure, like the Indian sari and the sarong. *Long diagonal lines bring length and grace to a woman's stature.* It automatically gives the illusion of height—similar to an asymmetrical one-shoulder dress or gown.

Shawls offer another opportunity for draping. You can wrap yourself in gossamer silk organza or the most luxurious pashmina to add grace and grandeur to your ensemble. It is most appropriate when you feel the need for modesty or to adhere to a religious tradition. A shawl is one of the most innovative ways to cover your arms, back, shoulders, and décolletage. One of the best ways to wear it is to wrap it twice around one arm to anchor it, drape it over the same shoulder and then across the back to the other arm, exposing one shoulder. Or simply swathe it around the body just above the elbows. *In general, one should avoid draping a shawl across both shoulders, as this often looks matronly.* This creates a strong horizontal line that is especially distracting in photographs when worn with casual insouciance, the wrap is elegant, functional, and feminine.

Madame Grès, the legendary Parisian couturière who was the queen of classical, Grecian–inspired draping, created masterful dresses in her Paris atelier from the 1930s through the 1970s. Not surprisingly, considering the elegant folds and curves of her dresses, Madame Grès was trained as a sculptor. Working the drape of her gowns in the finest silk jersey, she invisibly stitched the softly pleated folds by hand, creating an unparalleled liquidity of movement, grace, and beauty.

One-shouldered silk gown by Madame Grès, photographed in the mirrored hall at Fontainebleau, Paris, 1952

Above: Silk jersey dress, Spring 2009 collection
Opposite: Satin and silk gown, Fall 2010 collection

Playful Pleating

Another wonderful way to achieve a sense of
elongation is with the clever usage of pleating.
This decorative form of fabric manipulation and
ornamentation became very popular in the
late 1800s as one of the signature styles from
the house of Fortuny. It became so iconic to that
design house, that this particular type of linear
and irregular pleating is now referred to Fortuny
pleating; however, there are many other types of
pleating methods that are utilized in fashion.

One of the most attractive types of pleating is
sun-ray pleating, or plissé soleil, where there
appears to be no visible girth to the top of the
pleated panel. The measurement of the pleat
becomes gracefully deeper as it approaches the
bottom of the panel, creating luxurious volume.
I usually employ this method of pleating for
skirted silhouettes in silk chiffon, because
it creates such magnificent movement.

Pleated silk organza one-shoulder gown, Fall 2007 collection

The Art of Asymmetry

Another fascinating element of design—and possibly one of the least rational—is the use of odd numbers. Although it may seem strange that designers gravitate toward the use of one or three buttons on a jacket instead of two, it does feel more balanced. *There is something strangely appealing about asymmetry—whether it be a one-shoulder dress or the askew drape of a bodice.* Perhaps this seemingly illogical design decision speaks to some subliminal part of our subconscious.

In Japanese aesthetic theory, an odd number of elements is more appealing to the eye because it emulates nature, where little is perfectly symmetrical. The odd-number design concept is used in many Japanese arts including ikebana, the intricate Japanese art of flower arranging. Ikebana derives its beauty from asymmetrical compositions—often consisting of three or seven stems—and a spiritual attempt to express a slice of nature. *Achieving the beautiful balance of perfect shape, proportion, and movement is the master plan of every fashion designer, and the foundation of all great design.*

Above: Pleated metallic lace one-shoulder dress, Spring 2008 collection
Opposite: Silk jersey gown, Spring 2009 collection

TIMELESS FASHION
From the Ball Gown to the
Little Black Dress

Certain silhouettes in fashion transcend time and are consistently glamorous. After all, the art is oriented around a specific form—the human body. There are certain elements of style that will always look graceful on the female form—a strand of fabulous pearls or a beautiful white blouse. But like seasons in a garden, fashion runs through its own cycles of regeneration.

It is said that the periodic ups and downs of skirt lengths reflect the changing moods of the stock market. I, for one, have never figured out what that means. Is a rising hemline a sign of prosperity, or the reverse? No matter. Trends in color and style are cyclical as well—sometimes recycled in three years as is the case with animal print—or five, seven, or ten years. For instance, the one-shoulder silhouette blossomed again in 2008 after almost two decades of dormancy.

Two-piece ball gown, Spring 2003 collection

The Ball Gown

The ball gown was the customary attire for social occasions from the 1850s to the 1920s, when it fell out of favor with the arrival of Madame Vionnet's revolutionary bias-cut designs. In essence, Vionnet emancipated women from the confines of the ball gown's corsetry and strenuous construction which had become de riguer for high society for over half a century. This sensuous silhouette stayed popular throughout the golden years of Hollywood, until Charles James masterfully resurrected the ball gown silhouette in the 1950s with a sculptural design that epitomized an era. *This silhouette remains popular to this day, because it is so flattering accentuating the waist and minimizing the hip.* I simply adore this silhouette for the most special of occasions, as there is so much history associated with its design.

Above: Dior's satin gowns of the 1950s epitomized the era
Opposite: Beaded lace and silk organza gown with ruffled skirt, Fall 2005 collection

The Party Dress

There are other classic shapes that regularly reinvent themselves to wonderful effect. The full-skirted party dress, evocative of Christian Dior's New Look from 1947, is one of them. Essentially a truncated ball gown, this beguiling silhouette is popular once again because of its figure flattering shape. I consider the shape to be flirtatious, feminine, and perfect for almost any occasion. I am so enchanted by its spirit, vitality, and joie de vivre. There is something so celebratory about the silhouette that I find it perfect for so many different affairs—from cotton piques and prints for casual afternoon luncheons to layers of tulle and lace in black or white with resplendent embellishment for the most splendid black-tie affairs.

Shredded chiffon party dresses, Spring 2011 collection

One-Shoulder Necklines

Personally, I love the one-shoulder style because of its classical origins. It dates back roughly five thousand years to the beginnings of civilization in both Mesopotamia and the Indus Valley. It is an extremely flattering style; the fabric traverses the body in one strong diagonal sweep while drawing attention upward toward the face.

Empire Waist

The empire style, which was most famously worn by Napoleon's wife, Josephine, is a perfect example of how fashion transcends time. *Although the Empress Josephine was petite, the silhouette elongated her body, visually changing the proportion of her figure.* And now, over a hundred years later, the empire waistline has become extremely popular again for the exact same reason—its ability to add height to the wearer.

Above left: Embroidered lamé baby doll dress, Spring 2007 collection
Above right: Satin face organza ball gown, Spring 2007 collection
Opposite: Black silk velvet and ribbon embroidered one-shoulder gown,
Fall 2005 collection

The Little Black Dress

There is no item in a woman's wardrobe that is as important as the iconic little black dress. This fashion essential was first introduced by the legendary Coco Chanel in the 1920s and highly embraced for its versatility and practicality. *Throughout the years, the dress silhouettes and fabrics may have changed, but the importance of the LBD remains.*

There are many shapes that reappear from time to time in fashion. Some stay in fashion longer than others and some simply become fashion staples, such as the sheath dress and the a-line. These timeless shapes, which were so popular in the 1950s have since resurfaced in a multitude of variations and colors.

Other shapes like the trapeze and the bubble resurface less frequently. These silhouettes might have a hiatus of thirty years, or an even longer period of dormancy. They might reappear in sequins or taffeta; however, there is nothing more elegant and timeless than when these classic designs are realized in black.

Chantilly lace cocktail ensemble, Fall 2002 collection

Above left: Wool sateen and corset detailed cocktail dress, Fall 2002 collection
Above right: Crystal beaded metal lace cocktail dress with wool sateen tuxedo jacket, Fall 2002 collection
Opposite: Silk velvet corset and silk velvet skirt with silk chiffon tiered hem, Fall 2002 collection

Embellishment

Embellishment is recycled, too. When Tina Turner made her comeback in
the late '80s, I created a lot of sequined and caviar-beaded micro-mini
dresses for her Private Dancer tour. Twenty years later, sequins shimmered
back into fashion, and we created a similar dress—a black sequined baby-
doll cut on the bias that proved very popular.

Above: Tina Turner's sequined trapeze cocktail dress, Fall 1990 advertising campaign
Opposite: Beaded devoré velvet (detail)

Above: Metallic chantilly lace gown with ruffled train, Fall 2005 collection
Opposite: Velvet and jet-embroidered silk moiré gown, Fall 2005

83

Vintage

What I adore about vintage clothing is the incredible workmanship that you find in so many of the pieces. *The designs alone can be so beautiful, but for me, it is really the details of these handcrafted garments that are the true works of art.* I love the bound buttonholes, the zippers that are set by hand, and the pinked seams. Many of the fabrics and embroideries of these vintage pieces can no longer be reproduced. And because of this unique and irreplaceable quality, vintage pieces are frequently worn on the red carpet.

Certain embellishments in clothing also transcend time. Beading and sequins first emerged in the Roaring Twenties with those fabulous flapper dresses. In the '50s the beadwork reinvented itself upon wonderfully embroidered twin sets, which are still amazing to this day. In the 80's, beads came back in vogue.

Fashion Staples

If you have an article of clothing that you simply adore and haven't worn for a while, there is no reason why it should not be revisited many years later. Just as with a friend that you haven't seen for some time, it is so nice to get reacquainted with classic, staple pieces. The same is true with vintage items—as long as you style the piece in a way that is current. *A black sequined miniskirt from the '80s, for instance, could look totally chic twenty years later with a simple tank or a long-sleeved cashmere sweater.*

Whenever a style is revived by a fashion designer, like the return of the mini or the shoulder pad, many women will say, "If you've worn it once, you should never wear it a second time." I totally disagree. Nothing in fashion ever returns as a literal translation of its previous incarnation. If it did, it would be a costume. The new versions are designed independently and worn differently in a spirit reflective of their time. Attitudes and accessories change, so the new look will never be an exact duplicate of the past.

Beaded lace and satin bias-cut gown, Fall 2004 collection

New York
Fashion's Edge

Many things in my life inspire me—my beloved weekend home in the Hamptons, the magnificent black irises in my garden there, the fascinating influences of other cultures, and, of course, the unparalleled energy of New York City. I love anything and everything about New York. For me, it is the constant reinvention and rejuvenation of this city that is so inspiring. It's the eclectic personalities of the neighborhoods, the exuberance of Times Square, and, of course, the excitement of New York Fashion Week. There are so many facets of New York City that never cease to captivate me, and therefore it is quite appropriate that the showroom where I create my collections is located on Seventh Avenue in the center of America's fashion industry.

I love New York because it's always evolving. Hell's Kitchen has become hip, the Meatpacking District chic, and Harlem is thriving. The development of the sports complex at Chelsea Piers has turned old shipping docks on the Hudson River into a major playground. Times Square went from gritty to grand in the 1990s and now boasts pedestrian plazas. And the Financial District is moving from strictly business into a twenty-four-hour neighborhood with apartments, restaurants, playgrounds, and other amenities.

Metallic cocktail dress woven with patent leather, Spring 2009 collection

New York is a constant source of inspiration because it's
so ethnically and culturally diverse. It's like a nation
unto itself. The density factor—sixty-seven thousand
people per square mile in Manhattan—is amazing.
Naturally, you see every imaginable style of dressing on
the street—sometimes amusing, sometimes trendsetting,
and occasionally utterly outrageous. It's one of the best
people-watching places in the world. It is also my home.

Above: Pewter leather embroidered cocktail dress, Spring 2009 collection
Opposite: Inspiration for Carmen's Spring 2010 collection: "The Urban Jungle"

New York Style

Every neighborhood in the city reflects its own unique style. Downtown, there's arty SoHo, the trendy new designer stores on Bleecker Street in Greenwich Village, and the ever-changing Battery Park area by Wall Street. Uptown, there's the elegance of the Upper East Side and the beauty of tree-lined Park Avenue, and there's always a new boutique opening on Madison Avenue. And then there is the majesty of Central Park, which I so adore. While my apartment in the city has views of the park, like many in New York, I live without private outdoor space, and have therefore come to view the park as my extended garden.

I so much love the sparkle of the city lights and the electricity of Times Square, all ablaze in neon, that for several seasons I have made the NASDAQ building the platform to showcase my collections to the press. I cannot explain what it feels like to have JumboTrons broadcast my work to everyone in Times Square. How glorious to see not only my collection but also my name fifteen stories high above the heart of Manhattan!

The pulse of the city, the symmetry of its streets, and the shine of its steel have served as a muse for one of my more recent collections. Dedicated to the urban warrior and inspired by the incredible intersections of the city, the collection captured the strength and beauty of the skyscraper in a monochromatic palette of black, granite, and glass. The collection epitomized the vitality, power, and vibrancy of the world's most amazing microcosm.

New York style is anything edgy . . . anything daring . . . anything unexpected . . . and always in black.

Opposite: Beaded lace ikat dress, Spring 2010 collection
Following page left: Metallic draped lace cocktail dress, Fall 2009 collection
Following page right: Petal lace and chiffon cocktail dress, Spring 2004 collection

Broadway Lights

At the crossroads of Times Square you will find the lights of Broadway, and it's always thrilling to be invited to the opening night of the talented women who wear my designs: Broadway legend Patti LuPone in *Gypsy*; Ashley Judd in *Cat on a Hot Tin Roof*; Jane Krakowski and the incomparable Chita Rivera in the revival of *Nine*; or Vanessa Williams in *Kiss of the Spider Woman* and *Into the Woods*. I love dressing these women for their red-carpet moments, but I love meeting these incredible leading ladies even more than that. Most recently, I had the privilege of meeting Angela Lansbury, and I have never been so starstruck. What an unforgettable experience!

Dressing for the premiere of a Broadway show can be exciting as well. There is an incredible sense of anticipation and energy that permeates the air. So one, really should dress the part for this opening night. *For these openings, cocktail attire is most appropriate for the attendee, but it should be something a little edgier than normally worn.* Try black. The signature color of New York City.

For the stars I always suggest something in color for their opening nights, something show-stopping. The fittings for these leading ladies occur in my carmine red showroom overlooking the Hudson River, just south west of Times Square. This is where the garments are created and tried on, where modifications are made, and where hundreds of photos are taken to ensure nothing is out of place.

Vanessa Williams attending the New York City Ballet Spring Gala, 2009

Fashion Week

New York Fashion Week is the industry's twice-annual extravaganza of runway shows. The spring collections are showcased in September, and the fall collections shown in February. There is so much excitement and anticipation leading up to Fashion Week, and so many late hours and sleepless nights. There are numerous fittings required and the casting of models to walk the runway. Sometimes it seems like an unimaginable amount of work for a mere fifteen-minute fashion show. But once each show is over, I cannot wait to begin work upon the next one. *I love Fashion Week—it's like opening night on Broadway for the fashion industry on Seventh Avenue.*

In recent years, the fashion community has contributed to the Red Dress Collection during New York Fashion Week to benefit The Heart Truth, a national campaign promoting awareness about the risks of heart disease for women. To increase the visibility of the cause, celebrities are invited to walk the runway wearing dramatic red dresses that have been specially created by respected designers. I have been involved with this show since its inception and have had the pleasure to dress many wonderful women for it. It is so rewarding to design a gown for a specific cause and for a specific individual. One year, the actress and model Carmen Dell'Orefice wore my flowing red gown with a matching floor-length cape. It was one of my most memorable moments—Carmen wearing Carmen!

Fashion is no stranger to charity. For as long as I can remember, the fashion industry has been a huge supporter of many organizations that support women's health. From Saks Fifth Avenue's Key to the Cure, to Fashion Targets Breast Cancer, to Super Saturday benefiting the Ovarian Cancer Research Fund, the fashion industry has heart and soul.

Opposite: Looks from Carmen's runway shows during Fashion Week.

Going Gala

The fashion industry's most celebrated partnership is with the annual Costume Institute Gala at the Metropolitan Museum of Art, an event that was first organized by the legendary fashion arbiter Diana Vreeland. This highly publicized evening has become a mainstay on the New York social calendar, attracting celebrity and royalty alike in a celebration of fashion. I love dressing women for this prestigious gala, and I was particularly enamored with a gown I chose one year for Katie Couric. *The dress for a gala demands drama and flourish.* A train makes for a silhouette that won't be overwhelmed by the massive granite staircase leading up to the museum. But the gown cannot be too long, or it could make it awkward for a woman to ascend and descend those steps. The black and ivory dress I chose for Katie was perfection because it met all the requirements, and she wore it beautifully.

For such formal affairs as the Costume Gala, the dress must be grand and regal to compliment the evening, and it takes a lot of time and planning to be that fabulous. However, that is not the case for the majority of New York's black-tie events. Many of these events are black-tie optional, which basically means that cocktail attire is totally appropriate. *For many working individuals attending these benefits, it is much easier to wear a chick black suit to the office and bring a festive top to be changed into for the evening's event.* Or, wear a dress, and accentuate it with a fantastic necklace or scarf, or change into a different pair of shoes for the evening's revelry.

There is so much to love about New York. We have amazing restaurants with celebrated chefs. It is home to some of the best museums and art collections in the world. We have the cultural assets of the performing arts at Lincoln Center and many spectacular landmarks, such as the Time Warner Center on newly renovated Columbus Circle. New York is home to some of the most creative minds in their respective fields. We have a dynamic, constantly changing city that is so stimulating to my work, which is also continually evolving. The city helps me keep my ideas new and fresh. As an artist, I consider this to be one of the most inspiring places to be.

Silk lamé halter gown, Spring 2010 collection

Above left: "Window" beaded cocktail dress, Spring 2010 collection
Above right: Beaded metallic lace cocktail dress, Spring 2010 collection
Opposite: Silk lamé halter gown, Spring 2010 collection

HOLLYWOOD
The Red Carpet Capitol

I love Hollywood's glamour and prestige—in America, Hollywood icons are our royalty. I first became enamored with talented and beautiful leading ladies as a child, and my admiration for them grew even greater as I began working in fashion. I am so thrilled when someone chooses to wear one of my designs on the red carpet, and I am happiest when I am not aware it is going to happen; then it feels like a gift from God. The anticipation of whether an actress will wear one of my designs is sometimes so stressful. Between her fitting and her arrival on the red carpet, anything can happen. I anxiously await her entrance and suddenly she appears—sometimes in another designer's gown. This has happened to me more than once.

The first time an actress wore one of my gowns to the Academy Awards, it took me completely by surprise. I was watching the Oscars and about to retire for the evening when Julia Ormond walked on stage wearing my dress. It was a black crepe gown with re-embroidered lace appliqué and an open, crisscross back—very simple and understated—and she looked divine. I felt so honored.

Since then I've had the pleasure to dress many lovely women for the red carpet—fantastic stars such as Kate Winslet and Catherine Zeta-Jones, Lucy Liu and the legendary Angela Lansbury, Beyoncé Knowles, Clare Danes, and others. I have met many of these women, but not all of them. Sometimes there are many levels of people in between—stylists and studios, occasioally even hairdressers.

Taylor Swift wearing a metallic embroidered cocktail dress at the 2009
BMI Country Awards

Radha Mitchell at the Finding Neverland *premier, Brooklyn Museum, 2005*

What to Wear, Where

What I love most is when I get to know these gorgeous women as individuals and not merely as the characters they portray. Truly knowing a woman allows me to better complement her personality and inner beauty.

My dear friend Vanessa Williams is simply stunning, and has such an incredible figure that she could wear almost anything and in any color. It's never a question of what she will look best in; it is a question of what she will *feel* best in.

When dressing Vanessa—or any woman—for the dazzling events in her life, there are three factors to consider: what she's worn in the past, color, and volume. *If you wore black to the last affair that you attended, you shouldn't wear it again—unless, of course, black is your color.* And if it is, go ahead and wear black, but do not repeat the silhouette. Color—and how flattering it is on you as an individual—is key to making both a striking entrance and a lasting impression. The third factor is volume—is the look grand with yards and yards of silk taffeta or simply romantic with layers of bias-cut chiffon that float with each step?

Remember, every dress conveys a unique personality, so always choose the dress that best complements the mood you'd like to display. Do you wish to portray a feeling of grandeur and royalty, or is your desired effect more winsome and ethereal? The perfect combination of color and shape can, in one breath, translate as seductress, siren—and star.

Alluring Necklines

As a designer, my job is to elongate the body as much as possible, to give it a long, vertical line. We all want to be taller and thinner, and I try to stretch the body and fool the eye. I always attempt to draw attention up to a woman's eyes, to her sparkle and soul. We all love the one-shoulder silhouette, and it's the diagonal line of the silhouette that leads the eye up toward the face.

Once while I was dressing an actress for the Oscars, we at first wanted her to wear a strapless gown because her shoulders were so lovely. But without the height to pull it off, bare shoulders can sometimes become a broad horizontal band that breaks the long, lean line that we always try to attain. So we refitted the same dress as a one-shouldered silhouette, and she instantly appeared to grow four inches—even without her Louboutins!

Deep, plunging necklines are amazing on most women because they accomplish that same sense of length. And they are flattering for all bust sizes. I have used this silhouette for many celebrities—Tyra Banks, Mariska Hargitay, and Catherine Zeta-Jones—all with much success.

One year, I dressed Queen Latifah for the Oscars in a strapless black silk moiré gown with a sweetheart neckline and a full skirt of diagonal ruffles. She thought she didn't want to wear black, but she chose that dress for Oscar night, and the next day there were delightful photos of her twirling on the red carpet. I was so pleased to see how happy she looked in that dress!

Kim Catrall wearing a plissé soleil *halter gown at the Kennedy Center Honors, 2004*

Celebrity Style Secrets

Working with Marcia Gay Harden is always a thrill because I love watching her choose a dress for an event. She has a discerning eye and is highly aware of her carriage and how each design moves and complements her physique. I adore dressing Marcia Gay Harden—not only because she's an accomplished actress but also because it offers me the opportunity to hear her voice, which sounds sometimes like a violin, sometimes like a flute.

Lucy Liu was photographed several years ago wearing my shutter-pleat dress with a leather waistband. That image appeared everywhere, and it kept resurfacing as "best black dress of the year," "best mini," and "best cocktail dress." It became one of those little shining moments in red-carpet history. As a designer, I constantly challenge myself to create things of beauty. I always strive to find new ways to inspire myself to make each collection new and fresh. This keeps my mind nimble, hopefully resulting in beautiful new creations.

Most recently, Taylor Swift presented me with an unusual challenge. She needed an elegant gown that could be effortlessly torn off during her performance at the Academy of Country Music Awards. The plan was for her to descend gracefully through the air on a platform, arrive on stage, and remove her dress to reveal another costume—singing all the while. We needed to create an angelic ivory chiffon gown that camouflaged not only a steel safety harness but also all of the Velcro running along the empire waistline. It was a feat of pure engineering to make that ivory crystal-and pearl-studded dress, and it worked perfectly!

I am so inspired by Hollywood that a few years ago, I designed a fall collection around iconic stars of the silver screen—Marlene Dietrich, Greta Garbo, and Jean Harlow. In the first part of the show, the palette was primarily black and white, an homage to the power of George Hurrell's portraits. The second half was full of electrifying color, symbolizing the advent of Technicolor films. It was a glorious collection, full of glamour with seductive, shimmery gowns of satin or sequins. It was a collection in which I sought to inspire and empower women to shine in their own spotlight. I have no doubt—my love for Hollywood will continue to inspire me for years to come.

H.R.H. Princess Madeleine of Sweden, 2003

Above left: Lucy Liu wearing a leather and crepe mini dress at the 2001 SAG Awards
Above right: Claire Danes at the Toronto Film Festival, 2007
Opposite: Emmy Rossum wearing a one-shoulder cocktail dress in micro-pleated lace, 2008

Top left: Angela Bassett wearing the signature "shutter pleated" strapless gown at the Legends Ball; Center: Kim Raver in a print silk mousseline gown at the Golden Globes; Top right: Queen Latifah wearing a black moiré taffeta and silk organza gown at the Academy Awards; Bottom left: Kathryn Morris in a tangerine silk mousseline gown at the Emmy Awards; Bottom right: Vanessa Williams wearing a print silk mousseline strapless gown at the NAACP Image Awards

Top left: Sheryl Crow in beaded empire cocktail dress; Top center: Eve wearing a silk blouse and pearl embroidered skirt; Right: Marcia Gay Harden wearing a silk grosgrain ribbon gown at the Tony Awards; Bottom left: Mary J. Blige wearing a silk organza party dress with a Russian sable shrug; Bottom center: Jessica Lange in a silk brocade bias-cut gown at the Golden Globes

THE POWER OF COLOR
Mood, Mystery, Magic!

Color has the ability to transform and energize the spirit. It reflects and evokes strong emotions, and it communicates different things to different people. Color conjures links to nature and cultural icons that are sometimes subliminal, sometimes more obvious. For a designer, it is an extremely powerful tool.

Personally, I am passionate about red—the color of romance and the heart, of the flamenco and roses tossed at the matador's feet. It is the color of congratulatory bouquets and the color of triumph. Such a bold and vibrant shade is not for the faint of heart. It is a color that speaks of mystery and danger, of seduction and love.

The dominant color at my New York showroom is a dark, jewel-toned carmine red that's almost a claret. It's a sophisticated color sweetened with pink undertones, but it feels sensuous, with enough brown in its composition to arouse mystery. It's a personal victory color for me. It symbolizes strength, hope, and life. It reminds me of the Japanese maple I planted one summer long ago. Color can arouse so many different feelings in people.

Opposite: Pleated silk organza "Noguchi" gown, Fall 2007 collection
Following: Red silk dresses, Fall 2004 and 2008 collections

Orange & Yellow

Orange is a color that looks great on so many different skin tones. For me, it evokes a sense of the Orient—of Buddhist monks, spice, and exoticism. I associate the color with clove, sandalwood, and jasmine. I associate it with the sense of smell.

Yellow is vibrant and exciting, the color of bumblebees, daffodils, and sunshine. It is the color of ripe lemons in trees along the Amalfi coast.

Yellow and orange are both citrus colors, simultaneously acerbic and sweet—always bold, sensuous, and enticing.

Opposite: Silk taffeta strapless ball gown, Fall 2010 collection
Following pages: Iridescent silk chiffon gown, Fall 2008 collection

Blue & Green

Blue is deliciously versatile—so flattering on any skin tone. Blue is a painterly hue. It's the color of landscapes, of sky and sea. There is something about it that is so soothing. Whether it is the clarity of cerulean or the richness and opacity of cobalt, I love swathing a woman in blue. Wearing blue is like taking a swim in the ocean. Blues are the colors of summer.

Green, the familiar color of botanicals, is so peaceful and serene. It calls to mind grottoes resplendent with foliage and ferns. While the soft, pale, and bright shades stemming directly from nature are simply stunning on redheads and strawberry blondes, these colors are difficult for most women to wear. However, with the addition of a whisper of brown, these hues of green instantly become more wearable. Shades of olive and khaki are wonderful, and brassy, metallic greens are gorgeous on most skin tones.

Silk lamé asymmetric one-shoulder gown (detail), Spring 2010 collection

Pastels & Neutrals

Powdery pastels are colors many should avoid. Their tones are too similar to many complexions and tend to resemble cosmetic shades, which are not usually flattering as clothing to wear. However, these pale colors can be absolutely arresting on darker skin tones and Nordic blondes.

By themselves, soft pinks and lavenders strike me as girlish, but when you sweeten and enhance these colors, they take on a life of their own and become totally beguiling. Vivid flamingo pinks and bougainvilleas in all their glorious variations are so beautiful and much more complementary to the wearer.

Neutrals speak to me of something vintage and heirloom—the color of lingerie or tattered antique lace. They are beautiful, but soft colors can be very tricky for evening wear. *Choosing a color that mimics the skin tone too closely may drain all of the color from a woman's face.* These shades are better suited as accents rather than the main color of the ensemble. However, a palette of neutrals is transformed into utter sophistication when the fabric has a pearlescent quality to it. This shimmer will bring color to the face and will make the neutral more palatable against the skin. Still, when in doubt, make soft blushes your last choice, unless they are partnered with midnight or chocolate.

Above: Satin and silk chiffon halter gown, Spring 2009 collection

Opposite: Silk organza rosette (detail)

Chocolate

Chocolate, which has become a neutral in the fashion world, is gorgeous with almost any color. It pairs beautifully with aquamarines, pinks, purples and lilac. It looks stunning with camel and those vintage powdery pastels. There is something very opulent about dark chocolate, and it's kinder than black when paired with another color. Pairing chocolate with any color renders the combination sophisticated and smart, whereas black can sometimes become too pungent and overshadow the look.

Basket woven silk chiffon cocktail dress, Spring 2009 collection

Black & White

I love the use of color in my designs, but that being said, I don't consider black and white to be fashion "colors," which change with the seasons. They are perennials—my go-to colors for every collection I design. Black and white look fabulous on everyone.

Black is timeless; it speaks of sophistication and simplicity at the same time. There is something urban about black, and perhaps that is why I embrace it in my work. *Black is the perfect base color from which to begin a wardrobe. It is simple to accessorize and a dream to travel with.* You can accent black with any other color in the spectrum, from a soft pastel to a vibrant jewel tone. I adore it paired with midnight blue for a business luncheon or an evening soirée. To me, there is nothing more chic than this combination.

White evokes images of purity, innocence, and spirituality. Because of this association, it's traditionally worn for funeral services in Asian cultures. For me, it renders images of freshly fallen snow and dainty snowdrop flowers heralding the arrival of spring.

Although ivory is closely associated with weddings in the West, I don't believe it should be restricted to bridal use. *I love ivory as a color, especially for black-tie affairs.* It is so unexpected. It is one of the colors that I most recommend for women who are chairing events or acting as hostess. *In a sea of homogenous black suits and dresses, a woman in an ivory dress will be noticed instantly.*

Black and white are both pure achromatic colors, and together they represent the highest form of contrast. These two colors are so perfectly paired that little can go wrong when combining them in any proportion.

Satin face silk organza "Magnolia" gown, Fall 2003 collection

Above left: Crepe gown with pleated chiffon inset, Spring 2006 collection.
Above right: Crepe and satin gown with Chantilly lace, Fall 2008 collection

Above left: Mini rosette appliqué brocade cocktail dress, Spring 2007 collection
Above right: Silk blouson top with pleated "petal" skirt, Spring 2007 collection

Above: Metallic embroidered cocktail dress—also worn by Taylor Swift, Spring 2009
Opposite: Matelasse and organza one-shoulder gown, Spring 2011 collection

THE WEDDING

Styling Your Ultimate Red Carpet Moment

In many of life's celebrations, there are traditions that should be honored, but there are also aspects that can be personalized to fit your style. A wedding gown falls into the latter category—the priority should be that your dress makes you feel incredibly special, not that it fits into narrow cultural confines. If you feel glorious in your gown, then your joy will be apparent to your friends and family both during the event and in the many photographs commemorating the occasion.

A wedding can be a vulnerable situation for the bride. Walking down the aisle with all eyes upon you can be such an intimidating experience. Choosing a dress that makes you feel beautiful will alleviate some of the anxiety. When you feel good about how you look in your dress, you will exude confidence, and your family and guests will bask in your radiance.

Weddings can also be fraught with tension for the mothers of the bride and groom. When dressing for this special day, mothers should be more concerned with what is flattering on them than with the palette of the bridal party. I always hear the adage, "The mother of the groom should wear beige." No, please no! I'd rather see her in a gorgeous color that is flattering to her skin tone, even if it goes against tradition or the color palette of the wedding. The color that she selects to wear can enable her soul to sing—or sink. In the end, it's the memory of how she felt—and the wedding photographs—that will be treasured keepsakes for many years to come. We all know those pictures will ultimately occupy a special place on the piano.

Crepe back and satin bias cut-gown, Fall 2004 collection

Choosing the Gown

Searching for the perfect dress can be a confusing, and, at times, over-whelming process. *A camera is an invaluable assistant in helping you narrow down the choices and make your final decision.* Simply have a friend photograph you modeling each of your favorite designs, and then begin the elimination process. This is exactly what I do when working with celebrities for their events. The camera offers a much more honest second opinion than any family member or friend. Its lens is far more sensitive and accurate than the human eye, and much more objective!

Discovering the perfect bridal dress is one of the most exhilarating moments in a woman's life. The wedding is a joyful celebration of the couple's romantic quest to find each other, and its tradition connects the bride to a legacy shared with her mother, grandmother, and other brides. The wedding gown symbolizes a future full of hope and happiness.

Envisioning oneself in the perfect gown can be a somewhat elusive task. *Should you float down the aisle swirling in silk chiffon? Should you wear a tulle and Chantilly lace confection?* Are you looking for something that's elaborately beaded and re-embroidered, or are you searching for the soul of simplicity? You may find yourself overwhelmed by the sea of silhouettes from which to choose. *Photographing yourself wearing various dress options will help you determine whether your selections reflect your personality and flatter your figure.*

Opposite: Satin face silk organza "Calla Lily" gown, Spring 2007 collection
Following: Matelasse and re-embroidered lace gown, Fall 2008 collection

Silhouette Selections

Many women fantasize about a Cinderella gown with a big full skirt or a train that goes on forever. But this silhouette can be extremely cumbersome and add too much volume to your frame—especially if you are of diminutive stature and the fabric is stiff, such as a duchess satin or heavy damask. If it is your heart's desire to have a fairy-tale wedding dress, choose fabric for this silhouette as carefully as you have chosen your Prince Charming. A modified ball gown with a narrow front and an exaggerated back is easier to wear for most women. It still exudes volume and drama, but it won't eclipse the woman wearing it.

For destination weddings, travel is involved for the bride and her guests—and for the dress as well. Keep this in mind when selecting your gown. I adore bias-cut satin and bias-cut chiffon gowns for these occasions, because they convey elegance along with a certain insouciance that's perfectly suitable for dozens of locations throughout the world. Modern wedding gowns come in many shades of white, ivory, and candlelight, but this wasn't always the case. If you're searching for something that's truly unique, you need only look into history or other cultural traditions for ideas and possibilities.

The bridal gown has experienced many transformations over time. In Roman times, women married in a yellow veil and a white robe belted with a complicated knot—hence the term "tie the knot." In the Middle Ages, Icelandic brides chose dresses in varying degrees of midnight blue velvet. In fact, up until the nineteenth century, most brides in Europe and America simply wore the best dress their families could provide—in almost any conceivable color.

The white wedding dress didn't come into favor until the latter half of the nineteenth century, after Queen Victoria was married in a white satin gown trimmed with spectacular lace—a break from the traditional royal silver—setting a major trend that continues to this day. *Brides of the early nineteenth century typically also wore their wedding gowns on special occasions during the first year of marriage.* I personally adore this tradition from the past, and I encourage woman to embrace it. Wearing your gown for a second time can feel like a renewal. It's a perfect metaphor for the celebration of life.

Contemporary Weddings

For modern weddings, fashion speaks a multicultural language. Our global exposure has become so vast that the rules and restrictions of years past are beginning to merge and evolve. *Now, many women are choosing colors that reflect their individual personalities and philosophies.*

In Singapore, truly a melting pot of many cultures, bridal traditions are diverse: Malays prefer bright, spirited colors like saffron or red; Indians, crimson and gold—hues they associate with luck and happiness.

The Chinese traditionally wear a lavishly embroidered cheongsam in vivid red—the color of joy and luck. For the ceremony, Japanese brides typically wear a pristine white silk kimono symbolizing purity, and then don a bright, elaborately embroidered brocade kimono for the reception.

Accoutrements

Despite the tradition, I am not a fan of the veil. It can be awkward and even lead to some unexpected mishaps. I've seen a father accidentally lift one from his daughter's hair—along with her hairstyle. I've seen a veil fall on the floor of the church. And I've seen one blow away! On a day that is so emotionally charged, the veil needs to be carefully considered for its practicality. My personal preference is to skip the veil in favor of a beautiful hairstyle with a few strategically placed flowers or an elegant hair clip.

Jewelry is the finishing touch to that perfect dress. A great pair of earrings will frame the face beautifully, bringing full focus to the wearer. Too much jewelry has the opposite effect, tending to distract the eye from the woman, especially if she is wearing a large necklace. The spotlight should be reserved for you, not your accessories.

Seashell embroidered bias tiered chiffon gown, Spring 2005 collection

It is wonderful and endearing to see brides prepare
for their weddings with growing excitement and joyful
anticipation. The fulfillment of finding your soulmate;
the pure joy of walking down the aisle with that
person, poised to share your lives; and the anticipation
of the fabulous reception that follows—these are
truly some of the best red-carpet moments in life.

Above: Ruffle-back jacquard cocktail dress, Spring 2008 collection
Opposite: Crystal pleated lace spiral seashell gown, Spring 2008 collection

Above left: Metallic embroidered sheath, Spring 2007 collection

Above right: Sequined and embroidered sheath, Spring 2007 collection

Opposite: Guipure lace dress with silk "Mikado" coat, Spring 2007 collection

Following left page: Caviar pearl and cut crystal embroidery (detail)

Following right page: Seashell embroidered bias-tiered chiffon gown, Spring 2005 collection

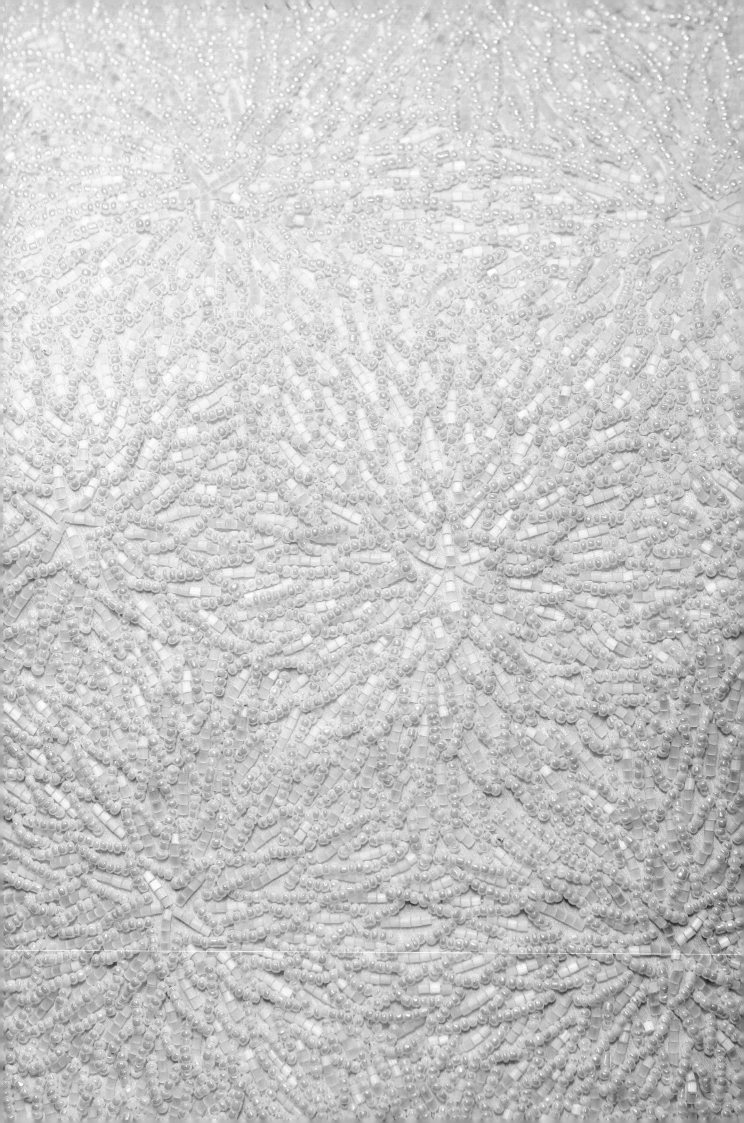

Above left: Silk satin face chiffon gown, Spring 2009 collection
Above right: Silk jersey asymmetric top and patent leather sequined skirt, Spring 2009 collection
Opposite: Silk moiré with re-embroidered lace inset gown, Spring 2009 collection

Above: Silk tiered organza one-shoulder gown, Fall 2009 collection
Opposite: Silk gazar cascade gown, Spring 2008 collection

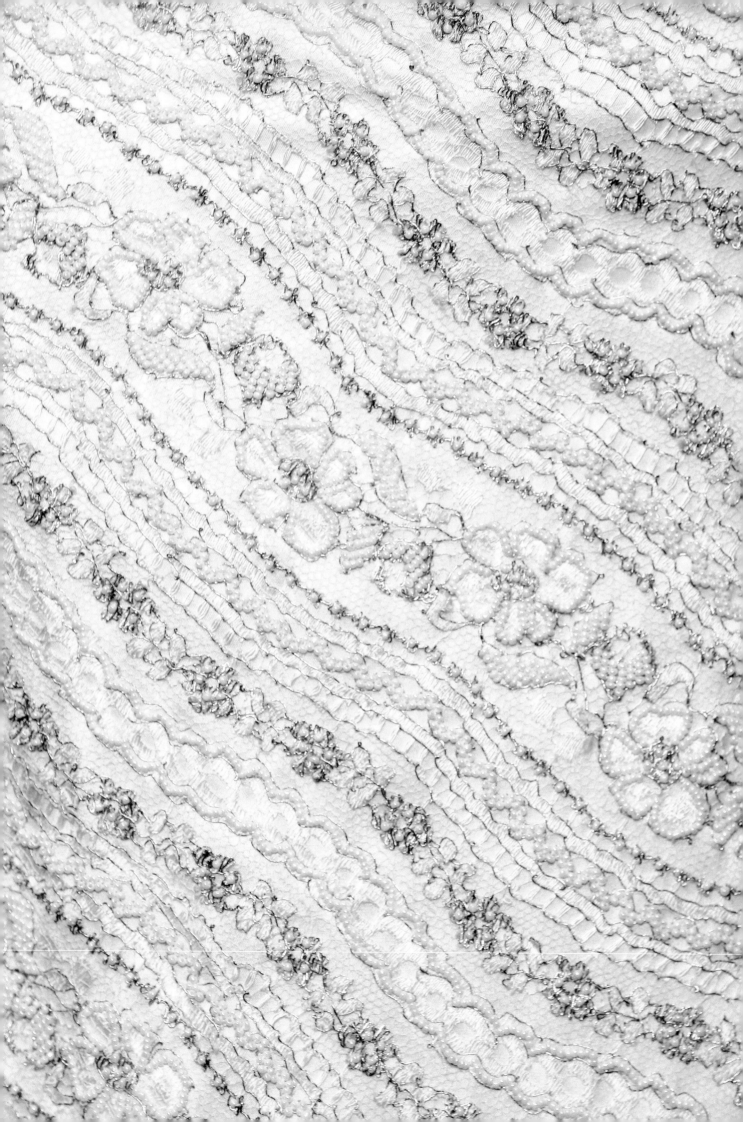

HAMPTONS CHIC
Summer Style

I love the color white. It's so clean and crisp, reminding me of summer in the Hamptons. If I had everything my way, the garden at our Bridgehampton home would be all white. But I admit that I adore the entire spectrum of color, so I plant colorful blossoms in the garden and I keep white flora blooming in the house. My indoor garden spreads throughout its rooms, with clusters of ivory-colored orchids encircling the white couches in the living room with its white walls and floors, and compact bouquets of pale cream roses on the coffee table. Nearby, clusters of white peonies decorate the table in the dining room.

I adore wearing white in the summer, when there is a certain casual ease to dressing. There is nothing so fabulous as a crisp white linen shirt worn with jeans and a great pair of sexy summer sandals. A white T-shirt worn with an embellished skirt is another example of warm weather perfection. It's the pairing of the simple wardrobe staple with the exceptional accessory or statement piece that should be summer's fashion mantra. Everything worn during these months should have a nonchalant air. Nothing should look formal or planned—your ensemble ought to have an air of spontaneity. To me, this is the epitome of Hamptons chic.

Silk organza strapless gown, Spring 2008 collection
Previous page left: Gold embroidered beaded lace (detail)
Previous page right: Beaded lace cowl-back gown, Spring 2010 collection

Chiffon Confections

During the summer, I especially like a dress made of chiffon—even more so when it's the color of white billowy clouds breezing across the bay on a lazy afternoon or when its movement has the energy of white-capped waves dancing the flamenco along the coastline in anticipation of a summer storm.

Chiffon is gorgeous when dappled with color. Chiffon infused with floral motifs has always been one of my signature ways to create a tableau of beauty on the wearer. I once photographed a bouquet of daffodils from my garden and then transferred that image onto silk. The ethereal quality of chiffon is perfect for so many summer soirées, especially garden weddings. I adore wrapping the body in cascades of silk chiffon ruffles on a bias-cut gown. Seeing a woman walk in this style of dress reminds me of a breeze wafting through a field of flowers.

I remember when we first explored the southeastern shore of Long Island to find our own patch of paradise. At the end of a narrow drive bordered by high hedges, we discovered a little guesthouse—a shack, really, with two bedrooms, one bath, and an outside laundry. But the location! It was spectacular—nestled right at the edge of wetlands thick with reeds and with a mesmerizing view of Mecox Bay. The property was practically barren—nothing but weeds and bad soil. It was the perfect canvas to grow a garden.

I'm not sure exactly when my garden started to become so important to me, but I took up the trowel around the same time that I launched a dress company under my own name. Perhaps, subliminally, the garden represented my new endeavor.

Printed silk mousseline bias-spiral ruffle gown, Spring 2011 collection

Above: Re-embroidered cotton guipure lace dress, Spring 2003 collection
Opposite: Floral prints, Spring 2005 collection

Blossoming Floral Prints

The flowers in my Bridgehampton garden have frequently inspired my collections, their glorious colors and patterns being the perfect genesis for summer prints. *I particularly love using floral motifs printed on a white background for shorter dresses; the look is fresh and appropriate for almost any summer event, from a casual luncheon to a more formal gathering.*

There is something very special about the frail, organic quality and texture of a blossom, a quality that has served as my muse on many occasions. The creamy peach and pink roses climbing around the columns on my front porch have inspired multicolored, floral silk organza flourishes on one of my favorite cocktail dress confections. I have also folded bias-cut strips of organza to create buds of peonies and roses on a gown.

My spring garden is ablaze with bright yellow daffodils—thousands of them. What a joyous sight after a long New York winter! As the daffodils begin to fade, my "blue" garden begins to replace it. It is a cool garden lush with lavenders and purples and a trace of pink. The perennial parade begins with the graceful wisteria that adorns the pergola by the pool. Then come the peonies and, finally, irises and foxgloves begin to punctuate the landscape during the long, dreamy summer.

Nestled between two gigantic weeping willows at the edge of the yard is the nearly hidden shade garden I created to escape the heat of the summer. It is truly the most relaxing place on the property, and where the sound of bamboo whistles in the wind. Hydrangeas and hostas abound, as do periwinkles, forget-me-nots, and violets. There is something quaint and simple about these flowering shade plants—they have an almost nostalgic quality. Their cool hues are complemented beautifully by the feathery greens of their fern companions. This combination of icy blues and rich purples with bright spring greens epitomizes the serenity of the shade garden, and I adore these colors on printed organza accented with silken florets.

Embroidered organza rossette (detail)

Above: Printed silk mousseline kaleidoscope gown, Spring 2006 collection
Opposite: Printed silk chiffon gown, Spring 2005 collection

A Garden of Inspiration

One year, when my health was not faring well, I created yet another garden. I removed much of the front yard and began to plant. It was a positive way to redirect my emotions and create a landscape of beauty with my own hands. Nurturing the plants—watching them grow and flourish—gave me a renewed sense of vitality and a feeling of hope.

My following spring collection was dedicated to that garden. Aflutter with layers of chiffon, ruffles, and flourishes, it was a collection that abounded in frailty and femininity as well as strength. It was about the triumph of the human existence, the wonderment of life, and the battle to overcome adversity.

The garden is a reflection of my soul. It is perhaps my most important muse and source of inspiration. It has helped me through many collections over the years, as well as many adversities. While I am stimulated by everything that surrounds me in this beautiful world—all of its wonders, cities, arts, and people—I do believe that, for most artists, nature is the ultimate source of inspiration. Just think of Van Gogh and his sunflowers and irises, and Monet with his water lilies or the abundance of landscapes that have been painted by so many different artists. There is a rhythm and progression to the garden that I find so moving. There is a heartbeat.

Ombre silk organza ruffle cocktail dress, Spring 2011 collection

Above: View from Carmen's home in Bridgehampton, New York
Opposite: Plissé soleil *baby doll gown, Spring 2006 collection*

Afterword

Life is a gift, a precious treasure that should
be cherished each and every day. Life is a time for
celebration, for enjoyment and for jubilation.

We should all strive to make each day a
memorable red carpet moment.

Taking time to smell the roses and peonies

lent perfume to daydreams of fantasy

a fairytale garden of good and temptation

a python coils through chiffon ribbons, cabbage

roses and petals glistening with morning dew

snakes coil encircling the hip and foot

morning glories caressing the bodies in layers of chiffon

nymphs gambol in verdant groves of blossoms

Carmen in his shade garden, Bridgehampton, New York

Dedication

I dedicate this book to my partner Christian,
who gave up his dream to share mine.

Bias-cut gown in black shadow stripe jersey, Fall 2003 collection

Acknowledgements

In any creative process, there are so many individuals who are intrinsic to the ultimate realization and success of any project, whether it be the creation of next season's fashions or embarking on a new project. This latest endeavor has been blessed with some amazing people who have helped me take this book from an idea to a reality. My heartfelt appreciation goes out to these extremely special people who have made this journey so joyous and memorable.

Firstly, to Katie Couric for honoring these pages with her beautiful foreword; for being such an amazing individual and an inspiration to so many, in so many different ways. Lisa Paulsen and Kathleen Lobb at the Entertainment Industry Foundation for all their invaluable work they do at the National Colorectal Cancer Research Alliance.

My dear friend, Vanessa Williams, for her years of support, not only for myself, but for all the foundations that are dear to my heart. You are a star in the truest sense of the word.

Dedie Leahy, my literary agent, the ultimate cheerleader. Thank you so much for your perseverance and your total commitment to this project.

Holly Haber, for her caring attention to detail, ensuring that my stories were properly conveyed and for her tutorage along the way.

The magnificent team at Rizzoli for their professionalism and impeccable attention to every detail: my publisher, Charles Miers, for believing in my vision and making it a reality; Ian Luna, for his interest and belief in the publishing of this work; Julie Schumacher, for keeping the idea alive until the right time appeared; Anthony Petrillose, for brilliantly overseeing the process with insightful literary expertise; Claire Gierczak, for her truly sensitive and eloquent gift as an editor; Allison Power for her diligence, unerring eye and excitement about this project and for always being there for me; Pam Sommers and Nicki Clendening for putting their genuine enthusiasm, as well as their exceptional skills into the publicity of this book.

My Carmen Marc Valvo family, including employees both past and
present, who give selflessly of their very being, enriching my life,
and allowing me to grow as a designer, including: Candy Chau,
without whom, I would be nothing; Frank Pulice, for his vision that
this book was meant to be from the beginning, and for all the years
he spent making it a reality; Il Park, my amazing creative director
and his incredible team, Giao Le and Elizabeth Santiago; Madeline
Twomey for her dedication; Jai Matthews and Taylor Foster, for
amusing me so many, many times; Kathlin Argiro, Tin Huynh,
Kazuki Kozuru, Don O'Neill, Ramin Paksima, Giancarlo Solimano,
Alan Tung, Cyril Verdevainne. And, of course, this would not be possible without Candy's amazing team, all of our pattern makers and
sewers and my production department for allowing my designs to be
realized so beautifully.

To my extended family and friends, especially my siblings: Lorenza,
Clarissa, Teresa, Anthony, and Christopher; all of my nieces and
nephews, and of course my parents, smiling down upon me from
up above.

The incredible artists that have graced these pages with their beauty,
talent, and artistry including;Joshua Allen for his early commitment
and input, Matthew Rolston for adding such power and prestige to
the project, and Melanie Dunea, for her amazing artistic interpreta-
tion and completion of this endeavor, my heartfelt thanks. Kevin
Aucoin, Frederick Boudet, Odile Gilbert, Ted Gibson, Franicis Hatha-
way, Romero Jennings, Carlo Longo, Vincent Longo, Tom Pecheaux,
Diego Da Silva, Charlotte Tiberus, Gucci Westman, for all their
talents. And all the incredible models and celebrities adorning this
book's pages, including: Eve, Angela Bassett, Mary J. Blige, Kim
Cattrall, Sheryl Crow, Claire Danes, Marcia Gay Harden, Ashley Judd,
Jessica Lange, Queen Latifah, Lucy Liu, Princes Madeleine, Maria
Menounos, Radha Mitchell, Kathryn Morris, Emmy Rossum, Kim
Raver, and Taylor Swift.

Photo Credits

p.4 (top left; right): JP Yim/WireImage/ © 2007 JP Yim; p.4 (bottom left): courtesy Carmen Marc Valvo; p.4 (bottom right): Frazer Harrison/ Getty Images Entertainment/ © 2008 Getty Images; p. 5 (left): Theo Wargo/ WireImage/ © 2010 WireImage; p. 5 (top center): Dan & Corina Lecca; p. 5 (top right; bottom): Frazer Harrison/ Getty Images Entertainment/ © 2008 Getty Images; p. 6: © Melanie Dunea/CPi; p. 8: Stephen Lovekin/ Getty Images Entertainment/ Getty Images © 2010 Getty Images; p. 11: Rabbani and Solimene Photography/ Wire Image/ Getty Images © 2007 Rabbani And Solimene Photography; p. 12: © Melanie Dunea/CPi; p. 15: Getty Images Publicity © 2005 Getty Images; p. 16–17: Tommy Agriodimas; p. 18: © Melanie Dunea/CPi; p. 20: © Everett Collection; p. 21: © 20th Century Fox/ courtesy Photofest; p. 22 (top left; bottom right; center): JP Yim/ WireImage/ © 2007 JP Yim; p. 22 (bottom left; top right): Fernanda Calfat/ Getty Images/ © Getty Images; p.23: Fernanda Calfat/ Getty Images © 2004 Getty Images; p. 24: © Melanie Dunea/CPi; p. 25: © Copyright 2010 Matthew Rolston Photographer, Inc. All Rights Reserved; p. 26: Philippe Halsman/Magnum Photos; p. 28: Frazer Harrison/ Getty Images Entertainment/ © 2006 Getty Images; p. 29: George Pimentel/ Wire Image/ Getty Images; p. 30: John Kobal Foundation/ Hulton Archive/ Getty Images; p. 31: Dan & Corina Lecca; pp. 32–37: © Joshua Allen; pp. 38–39: JP Yim/ WireImage/ © 2007 JP Yim; p. 40: © Melanie Dunea/CPi; p. 41: © Joshua Allen; p. 42: courtesy Carmen Marc Valvo; p. 43: JP Yim/ WireImage/ © 2007 JP Yim; p. 44: photograph Ruven Afenador, courtesy Bergdorf Goodman; p. 45: Dan & Corina Lecca; p. 47: © Joshua Allen; p. 48: Mark Mainz/ Getty Images Entertainment/ © 2007 Getty Images; p. 49: Frazer Harrison/ Getty Images Entertainment/ © 2006 Getty Images; p. 50: Raymond Meier/ Trunk Archive.com; pp. 52–53: Mark Mainz/ Getty Images Entertainment/ © 2007 Getty Images; p. 55: © Joshua Allen; pp. 56-57: Frazer Harrison/ Getty Images Entertainment/ © Getty Images ; p.58: © Condé Nast Archive/CORBIS; p. 59: © Copyright 2010 Matthew Rolston Photographer, Inc. All Rights Reserved; p. 60: © Condé Nast Archive/

Satin face silk organza "Magnolia" gown, Fall 2003 collection

Finale, Spring 2009 collection

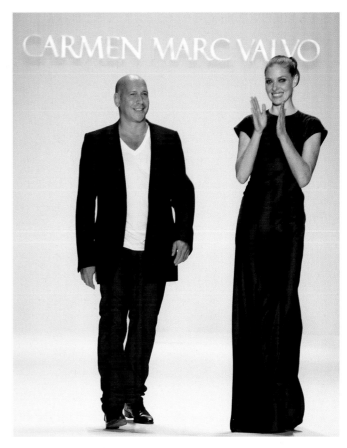

Finale, Spring 2009 collection

First published in the United States of America in 2011
by Rizzoli International Publications, Inc.
300 Park Avenue South, New York, NY 10010
www.rizzoliusa.com

© 2011 Carmen Marc Valvo

Design: Ellen Nygaard
Editor: Allison Power
Rizzoli Design Coordinator: Kayleigh Jankowski

2011 2012 2013 2014 2015/ 10 9 8 7 6 5 4 3 2 1

Printed in Singapore

Paperback ISBN: 978-0-8478-3614-7
Hardcover ISBN: 978-0-8478-3541-6
Library of Congress Number: 2010937589

Pages 4–5: Runway looks, Fall and Spring 2001–2010 collections